creative weaving

Sarah Howard and Elisabeth Kendrick

LARK BOOKS

A Division of Sterling Publishing Co., Inc.

New York / London

Library of Congress Cataloging-in-Publication Data

Howard, Sarah, 1955-
Creative weaving/Sarah Howard and Elisabeth Kendrick– I.
        First ed.
            p. cm.
        Includes index.
        ISBN-13: 978-1-60059-098-6 (pb-with flaps : alk. paper)
        ISBN-10: 1-60059-098-5 (pb-with flaps : alk. paper)
        1. Hand weaving. 2. Textile fabrics. I. Kendrick, Elisabeth, 1950- II.
Title.
        TT848.H665 2007
        746.1'4041–dc22

2007001952

10 9 8 7 6 5 4 3 2 1

First Edition

Published by Lark Books, A Division of
Sterling Publishing Co., Inc.
387 Park Avenue South, New York, N.Y. 10016

First published 2007
Under the title CREATIVE WEAVING
By Gaia (an imprint, part of) Octopus Publishing Group Ltd
2–4 Heron Quays, Docklands, London E14 4JP

© 2007 Octopus Publishing Group Ltd
All rights reserved
Americanization © 2007 Octopus Publishing Group Ltd

Distributed in Canada by Sterling Publishing,
c/o Canadian Manda Group, 165 Dufferin Street
Toronto, Ontario, Canada M6K 3H6

If you have questions or comments about this book, please contact:
Lark Books
67 Broadway
Asheville, NC 28801
(828) 253-0467

Manufactured in China

ISBN 13: 978-1-60059-098-6
ISBN 10: 1-60059-098-5

For information about custom editions, special sales, premium and corporate
purchases, please contact Sterling Special Sales Department at 800-805-5489 or
specialsales@sterlingpub.com.

Contents

Loom weaving

Weaving is the interlacing of two sets of threads, arranged at right angles to each other, in order to create a fabric. One set is called the warp – these are the lengthways threads that are held under tension on the loom. The other set is the weft – the yarn woven crossways through the warp to make the cloth. In this section we will show you how to get set up and start weaving on a rigid heddle loom. This is a simple, portable loom on which you create woven fabrics using plain (tabby) weave.

The weaving process

A loom is a stationary device for holding the warp threads taut so that you can weave the weft through them to make a woven fabric. Other parts of the loom are there to help make this process possible.

In plain (tabby) weaving the warp is threaded through the holes and slots of the reed, which is the central section of a device called the heddle (see page 5). The weft thread goes over and under alternate warp threads (*ends*) that are raised and lowered using the heddle.

Each time the heddle is raised or lowered, the weft, which is wrapped around a shuttle (see page 16), is passed through the space created (called the *shed*).

RIGID HEDDLE LOOM

The frame of the loom holds a front and back roller with sticks attached to which the warp is tied. The back stick and the warp are wound around the back roller when you set up the loom; the front stick and the completed fabric are wound around the front roller as you weave. At either end of the loom on the right-hand side are the ratchets and the ratchet brakes. These hold the rollers in place and keep the warp at the correct tension. Releasing both the brakes allows you to wind forward the woven fabric and unwoven warp.

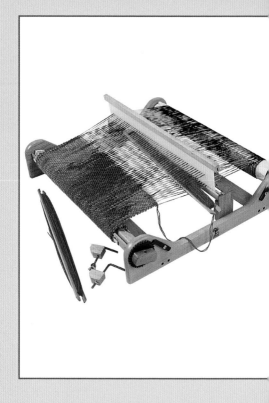

THE HEDDLE

The heddle raises and lowers the warp, creating a space (the *shed*) for the weft to pass through. When the loom is set up and during times when you are not weaving, for example when winding the woven fabric on to the front roller, the heddle sits in the heddle holders (see below) in the *resting position*.

When you set up the loom the warp is threaded through the holes and slots of the reed, the part in the heddle that spaces the warp threads (*ends*) and keeps them separate.

Heddles come in different sizes, measured as dents per inch (dpi) or dents per 10 centimeters. The dent refers to the warp spacing, which is governed by the number of holes and slots along the reed. If there are 40 dents in 4 inches, then this is expressed as 10 dpi (40/10 cm).

When weaving with thick yarn you use a heddle with a low number of dents, for example 5 dpi (20/10 cm). For fine yarn choose a heddle with a high number, for example 12 dpi (48/10 cm).

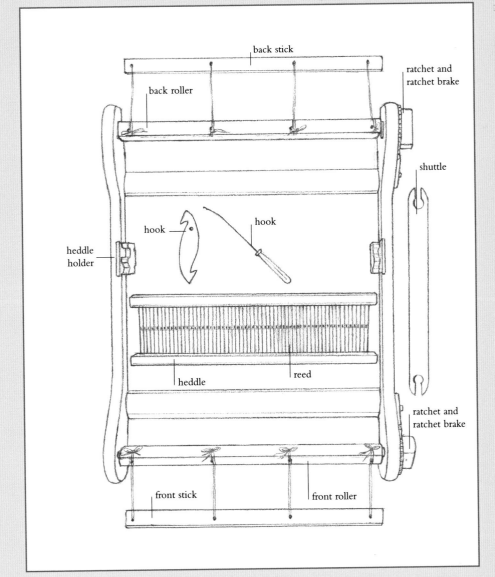

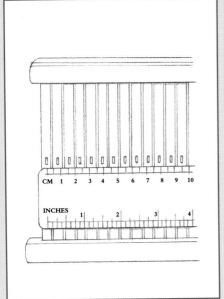

Yarn basics

Yarn is a general term given to fibers and filaments that have been twisted together ready to be used for many crafts including weaving, knitting and crochet. The projects in this book use yarns made from plant, animal and synthetic fibers, as well as fun materials such as wrapping paper and plastic bags.

The varying thicknesses and weights of yarns will affect the look, feel and flexibility of a woven fabric. Animal fibers, such as wool, mohair and alpaca, are warm to touch and have elasticity; silk has luxurious qualities, high luster but little elasticity; and plant fibers, such as cotton, linen and hemp, are cool to wear but lack elasticity. Synthetics, such as nylon, acrylic and viscose, are often added to other fibers to give sparkle and durability.

The standard terms used to describe the thickness of yarns are superfine, fine, light, medium, bulky and super. Yarn is also referred to as sport, DK (double-knitting) and chunky (see page 7, Yarn guide). It is the thickness of the yarn that will decide the size of the heddle required (see page 5) and ultimately the finished texture and feel of a woven fabric.

Yarns can also be described as 2, 3 or 4 ply. Ply is another word for strand or thread, so 4 ply is made up of 4 strands that have been twisted together to make a standard thickness.

Throughout this book you will find clear instructions to help you use the correct yarns for each of the weaving projects. You will also find a life-sized swatch of the warp and weft yarns with each project to enable you to use other yarns of your choice of a similar thickness.

WASHING THE FABRIC

Washing helps to close up the open texture of the woven cloth, allowing the threads to cling together. This gives the finished fabric its drape and flexibility and allows for any shrinkage to take place, which is especially important if the fabric is to be used for clothing. Follow the washing instructions on the yarn label or wash the fabric by hand, keeping the water temperature constant for both washing and rinsing. Dry flat.

 Tip Many yarns have the yardage printed on their label. Finer yarns will go further by weight than thicker ones.

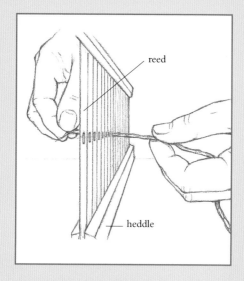

reed

heddle

WARP YARNS

The warp yarn must be suitable – not too thick and not too thin – for the reed. Also, it must be strong enough not to break when under tension. You can test your yarn by threading a piece through a hole in the reed and pulling it back and forth. A suitable yarn will flow easily without sticking, breaking or shredding. You can successfully mix different yarns in the warp, but you must distribute them evenly across the warp width making sure both edge (*selvedge*) yarns match. For a balanced weave without gaps use consecutive holes and slots.

The warp stretches when it is attached then tightened (*tensioned*) on the loom, but it relaxes as soon as the finished fabric is removed. This difference in length is called the *take-up* (see How much yarn?, page 7).

How much yarn?

Working out how much warp yarn to buy requires some simple arithmetic. The amount of weft yarn you need will be roughly the same, if the yarns are similar. Each project presented in this book tells you the type and thickness of warp and weft you will need. However, if you would prefer to use other yarns, the warp and weft for each project are shown as life-size swatches, so you can compare your chosen yarns to ours to see if they are suitable.

Wraps and reeds

Winding your warp and weft yarns together around a ruler creates a wrap. Making a wrap tells you the reed size that you need for a balanced weave (one that has an equal number of warp and weft threads in the finished fabric). Take one warp and one weft thread and wind them together around 1 in (2.5 cm) of a ruler, with the threads lying flat and close to each other. The ruler should not show between the threads and the threads should not overlap. Now count just the warp threads (*ends*) to find the reed size. For example, 5 wraps of the ruler will mean 5 individual warp ends per inch of weave or 20 individual warp ends per 10 cm of weave – 5 dpi (20/10 cm) reed.

WARP CALCULATIONS

The length of each individual warp thread (*end*) will be the length you want the finished piece to be, plus an extra 10% for the take-up. Then you need to add on enough extra to tie the warp onto the loom, specifically the front and back warp sticks. This is known as the loom allowance, and is about 24 in (60 cm) for an average rigid heddle loom.

To find the total number of ends, multiply the required final width of your finished piece by the reed size you found from your wrap (see left).

Finally, calculate the total warp length by multiplying the length of a single end by the total number of ends required.

Sample calculation

For a finished piece 30 in (75 cm) long and 12 in (30 cm) wide, using

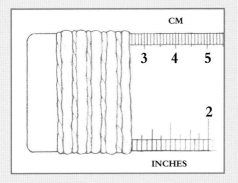

a 5 dpi (20/10 cm) reed, each end would be:
finished length 30 in (75 cm)
+ 10% for take-up 3 in (7.5 cm)
+ loom allowance 24 in (60 cm)
= total (rounded up) 57 in (143 cm)

The number of ends would be:
12 x 5 dpi (30 x 20/10) = 60

The total warp length needed is therefore 57 in x 60 (143 cm x 60) = 95 yards (86 metres)

Yarn guide

US	UK	Wraps per inch	Wraps per cm	Suggested reed size US	UK
Fingering, superfine sock	3 ply	20 wpi	8 wpc	12 dpi	48/10 cm
Sport, fine	4 ply	18 wpi	7 wpc	10 dpi	40/10 cm
Light worsted	DK (double knitting)	15 wpi	6 wpc	7.5 dpi	30/10 cm
Bulky	Chunky	12 wpi	5 wpc	5 dpi	20/10 cm
Super bulky, rug	Super chunk	8 wpi	3 wpc	4 dpi	16/10 cm

Winding the warp

Having calculated your warp yarn you need to prepare it for threading up your loom. To do this you will need either a warping board with pegs set around the edge (as shown here) or a set of warping posts with clamps that you attach to a table top. When preparing the warp you first measure out one warp end against the pegs using a piece of yarn that is equal in length to one warp end. Having done this you then wind the warp. Your measured warp is wound back and forth around the warping pegs in a continuous length, without breaks or knots. Path A to J, as shown below, is equivalent to the total length of one warp end including loom allowance and take-up (see page 7). If the total length of a warp end was shorter, then the last peg might be post G, for example.

Tip If you add on more warp yarn or change colors, make the joining knot at the beginning or the end of a warp thread at posts A or J. Knots in the middle of the warp may catch when weaving and cause the warp to break.

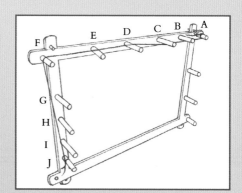

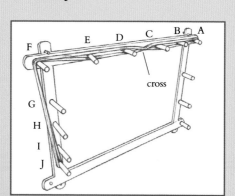

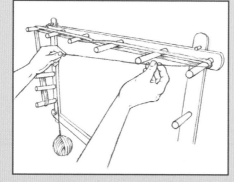

1 To set the warping board pegs in the correct place, use a piece of string or yarn measuring one warp end plus a little extra to secure it to the two end posts. Tie one end of the yarn to peg A, then guide the piece of string around the pegs following the exact path of the warp – this will include creating a cross between pegs C and D (see step 2). Move the pegs into position so that the distance from peg A to peg J is the length of a single warp end.

2 Starting at peg A, carry your warp yarn around the pegs until you reach peg J. Go around peg J and take the warp back to peg A.

The warp yarn should make a cross between pegs C and D on each journey of the warp, both going from post A to post J and coming back. To do this, take the warp below peg D on the forward journey and below peg C on the return journey. This cross keeps the warp ends in the right order for threading the heddle and also prevents them from tangling.

3 To maintain an even tension as the warp passes around the warping pegs, hold the yarn in your right hand while pulling the wool from the ball with your left hand. The warp does not have to be kept tight, but the tension should be even. Position your warping board at a good and comfortable height as the winding takes time.

COUNTING THE THREADS

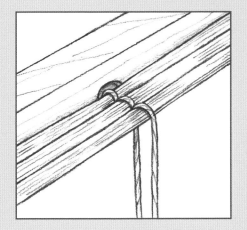

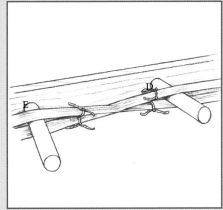

cross-sticks

4 To keep track of how many thread ends you have wound around the pegs you will use a *counting thread*. This is a length of scrap yarn that you wind around every 10 threads.

After you have wound the first 10 warp ends around the pegs hang your counting thread over the warp. Wind on a further 10 warp ends, then take take the counting thread and wrap it around the newly wound ends. Do this every 10 threads, until you have wound on all of the warp.

5 When all the warp is wound, secure the cross between posts C and D (see page 11) by tying pieces of contrasting color thread around each grouping of warp threads (*ends*) on either side of the cross. Use a different colored thread from the counting thread so that you can easily see which is which when you are threading up.

6 Continue securing the warp at regular intervals with a contrasting thread until the entire warp is securely held. Now insert the two cross-sticks that were supplied with your loom, one on each side of the cross between posts C and D. Tie their ends together. The cross-sticks are used to help keep the wound warp in order when threading the heddle (see page 11).

 Tip A counting thread helps you to see at a glance how much warp you have wound onto the warping board. Use a scrap piece of yarn in a bright contrasting color.

REMOVING THE WARP

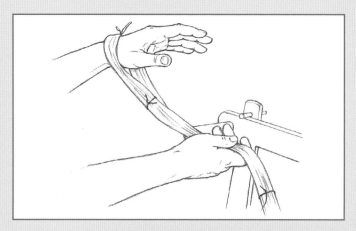

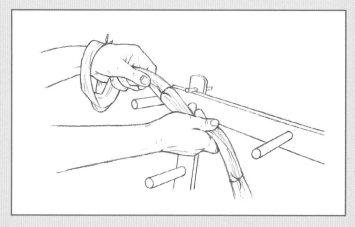

7 Now remove the warp from the warping board and make a chain with the warp. To do this lift the warp from post J, put it over your left wrist and hold a length of the warp loosely in your right hand. This end of the warp is the farthest end from the cross and will be tied to the front stick on the loom (see page 4).

8 Take hold of a length of warp with your left hand while still holding on to the warp with your right hand.

9 Now use your right hand to slide the loop of warp off your left wrist and over your left hand to make a new loop. Put this new loop over your left wrist, and continue this process to make the chain. Once you are near the cross-sticks (peg D) stop chaining and remove the remaining warp and the cross-sticks from the warping board. Your warp is now ready to put on the loom.

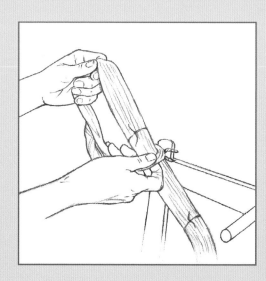

Setting up the loom

There are four distinct processes when setting up the rigid heddle loom –
threading the heddle (steps 1–5), tying the warp to the back stick (step 6),
winding on the back roller (steps 7–10) and tying the warp onto the front
stick. With practice you will be able to put the warp on your loom on your
own; however, for the first few times you may find it easier to have someone
else help you.

THREADING UP

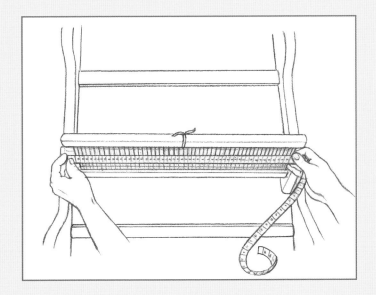

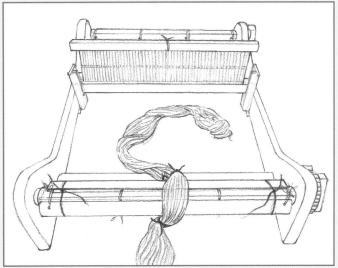

1 To make sure the warp is spread evenly across the
heddle, find the center point of the heddle using a
measuring tape as a guide. Mark this point with a piece
of thread of a contrasting color.

2 Tie the cross-sticks to both ends of the front roller with
a spare piece of yarn – this will keep the warp secure
while you thread up. Make sure the warp chain is
supported on the table. The end of the warp closest to the
cross you created between pegs C and D on the warping
board (peg A, see page 8) will be threaded through the
heddle and tied to the back stick. Remove the cross ties
(see step 5, page 9).

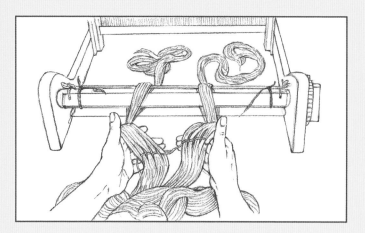

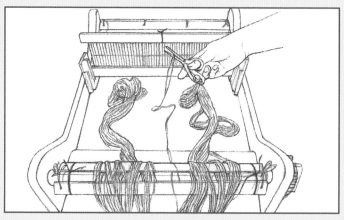

3 Using the counting thread as a guide, find the center of your warp and gently part it from the counting thread through to the end of the unchained section of your warp.

4 Keeping the center of your warp clearly visible, spread the warp ends along the cross-sticks across the entire width of the loom. Each pair of warp ends should be visible, ready for threading. Then, working from the center outwards, take each pair of warp ends in order and cut the loop to make two separate warp ends.

5 Working from the center of the heddle outwards use your threading hook to thread the warp through the holes and slots of the reed. Take each warp end from the cross-sticks in consecutive order, the over thread then the under thread. All over threads go through the holes and all under threads go through the slots, for example. To create a balanced plain weave each slot and hole should be used. Finish with a pair of warp ends in the last hole or slot, to help form a firm edge (*selvedge*). Repeat this process across the other half of the heddle, again working from the center to the edge of the loom.

Tip If your heddle is fine, with a high number of dents per inch or dents per centimeter, you may need to use a threading hook to thread the yarn.

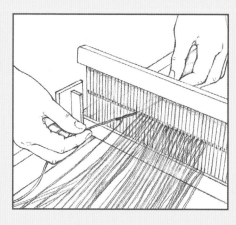

TYING TO THE BACK STICK

WINDING ONTO THE BACK ROLLER

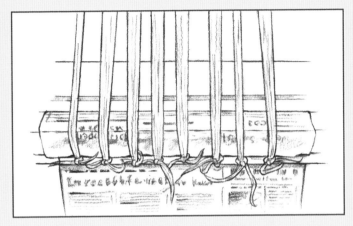

6 Now tie the warp ends to the back stick. Starting at the center of the warp and working outwards, divide the ends into small bunches of 6, 8 or 10 threads. Wrap each bunch of ends around the back stick, then as you bring the threads up, split them into two groups on either side of the warp and tie them in a double knot over the top of the warp ends. Once all the ends are tied to the back stick turn the ratchet until the back stick sits on top of the back roller.

7 Before you begin to wind the warp onto the back roller (*to position*) untie the cross-sticks from the front roller and remove them from the warp. Take the first numbered sheet of newspaper (see tip box, below) and make sure it is wider than the width of the warp but not as wide as the loom. Slip the edge of the newspaper under the back roller then up between the back roller and the warp ends.

Tip Sheets of newspaper are used when winding onto the back roller to help prevent the warp ends from tangling and to help keep tension. Number the sheets of paper as you wind, as this will help you to calculate later on how your weaving is progressing and roughly how much you have left to do.

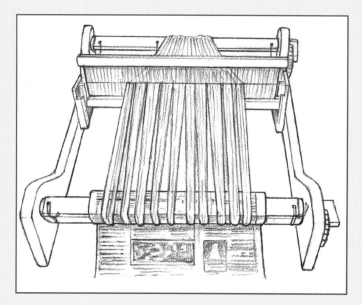

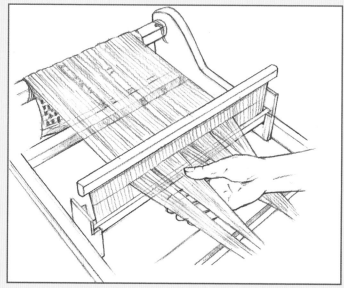

8 Now start to wind the warp onto the back roller by turning the ratchet (see page 18). Undo the warp chain, removing any ties and the counting thread as you go, making sure that the warp remains smooth and untangled. Roll the newspaper on at the same time, adding a new sheet as required.

9 As you wind on, smooth the warp ends from the front of the heddle with your other hand. Every few turns, check that there is no snagging in the heddle and the tension is even.

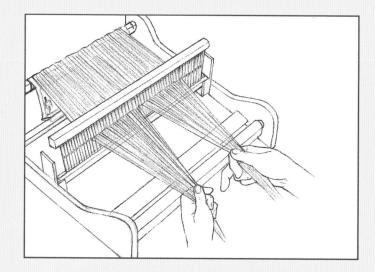

10 Continue winding until most of the warp is on the back roller, leaving approximately 15 in (40 cm) at the front of the heddle to tie securely to the front stick.

TYING TO THE FRONT STICK

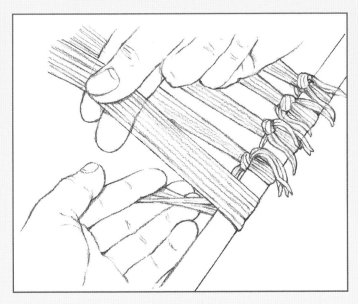

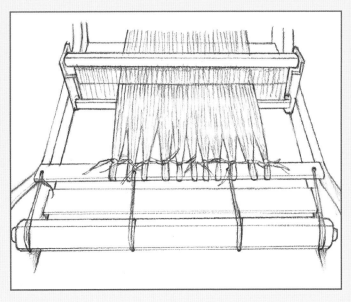

11 Next you need to tie the warp ends to the front stick. Working from the center of the warp, take small bunches of 6 to 10 warp ends and smooth them through your fingers before taking them over and around the front stick.

12 Begin to knot the bunches to the front stick as you did on the back stick (see page 13), but use a single knot only. Work from side to side to maintain an even tension.

 Tip Adjust the warp ends where necessary by untying the knot and pulling up the slack before retying.

13 When all the threads have been tied, return to the center knot and begin again. Check each bunch, retightening by lifting and pulling the knot towards the heddle to take up any slack. Then secure with a double knot. Test for even tension by gently patting the warp ends with the palm of your hand.

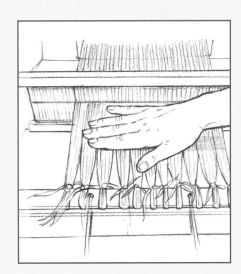

Plain weaving

Once you have learned the basic plain (tabby) weaving technique, you will be able to go on to add embellishments and patterns to your woven projects (see pages 22–24). As you become more practiced you will find the separate stages of plain weaving become one continuous movement and your weaving will get much quicker.

When you start off your weaving project the first thing you do is to make the header out of a thick yarn in a contrasting color (see page 19). The header is also woven using plain weaving, as described here.

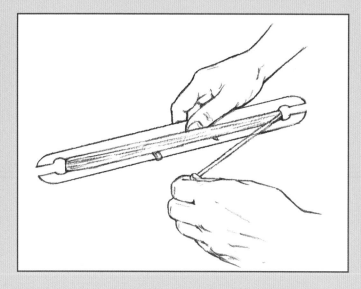

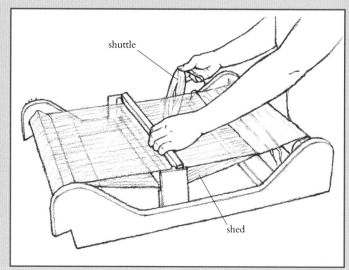

1 Wind the weft evenly around your shuttle (see page 4). Avoid overloading it as the shuttle must pass easily through the shed – the space created when you raise and lower the heddle. If you want to experiment with different weft yarn combinations you will need to wind a separate shuttle for each weft.

2 Take the heddle out of the heddle shafts (*rest position*) and lower it into the down position to create a shed between the warp ends. As you lower the heddle the warp ends threaded through the slots in the reed will move up to the top of the heddle. Slide the shuttle through to the other side, leaving the loose end to be trimmed later.

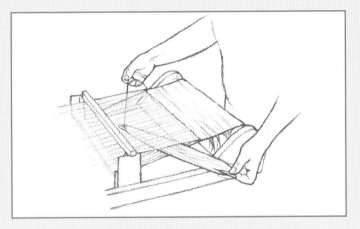

3 Ensure that you don't pull the weft too tight, by making an arc shape with your weft yarn before pulling the shuttle gently out on the other side (see page 19).

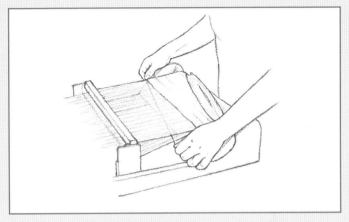

4 Put the shuttle down, hold the weft with both hands and pull it towards you. Check that the edges (selvedges) are even and not pulling in or forming straggly loops (see Keeping an even selvedge, page 20).

Tip Try to develop a regular rhythm through these five steps to produce an even weave.

5 Remove the heddle from its resting position holding it firmly from the top with one hand at either end. Bring it towards you and use it to push the weft evenly into place. This process is called beating.

Now repeat steps 2 to 5 with the heddle raised in the up position. The warp ends threaded through the slots in the reed will now move down to bottom of the heddle.

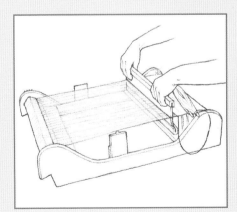

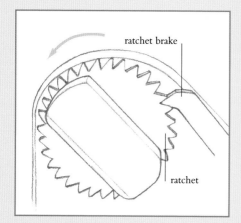

ratchet brake

ratchet

6 Continue with steps 2 to 5, until you no longer have a wide enough shed to pass the shuttle through. To wind on, put the heddle in the rest position and release the ratchet brakes. Turn the ratchet brake on the front roller and roll on the woven fabric until its edge is 2 in (5 cm) from the front roller. Secure both ratchet brakes and adjust the tension, which should be firm but not tight. When the weft yarn runs out, wind the shuttle as before (see step 1). Join in the new weft thread (see page 21) and continue weaving.

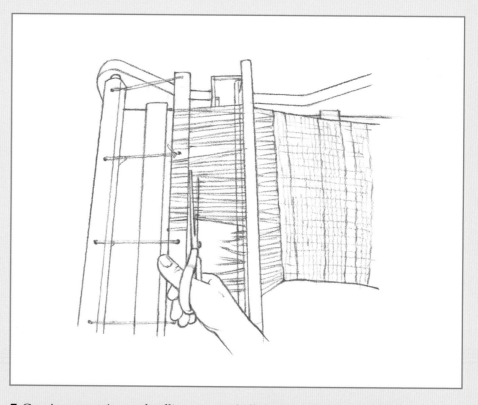

7 Continue weaving and rolling on until all the warp has been used. When you have finished weaving, place the heddle in the rest position and release the ratchet brakes on the front and back rollers. Cut the warp off the back stick and pull the warp ends through the heddle. Unroll your weaving from the front roller and cut the warp from the front stick. Remove the header one row at a time. You can now secure the raw edges with a sewing machine stitch sewn alongside the first and last rows of weaving. Any remaining warp can be cut away or used to make a fringe (see page 22).

Auxiliary techniques

To successfully create a variety of woven fabrics on your rigid heddle room there are a number of additional techniques you should know. These techniques will help you become a proficient weaver.

MAKING THE HEADER

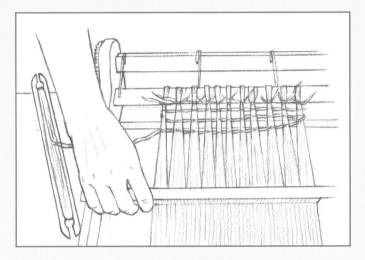

When you start any weaving project on a rigid heddle loom you begin with making the header. Its purpose is to open up the bunches of warp ends created when you tied the warp to the front sticks (see page 15) and to close the gaps between the bunches. The header is discarded when the woven piece is finished.

Use a thick yarn in a contrasting colour. Weave the first three rows with plenty of slack in them before beating into place (see pages 16–17). Then weave another six or eight rows, beating each row firmly. Hold the heddle firmly with both hands, from the top at either end, so that the pressure of the beat is spread evenly along the weft as you pull it towards the front roller with a swift, firm movement.

ARCING THE WEFT

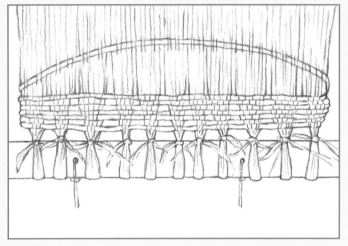

When you pass the shuttle through the shed, leave the weft lying in a single arc before beating it in evenly with the rigid heddle. This gives the weft the little extra length it needs to be able to lie over and under the warp ends. Without it your weaving will gradually draw in at the sides and get narrower.

KEEPING AN EVEN SELVEDGE

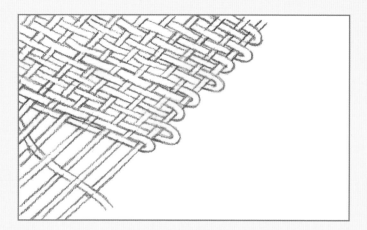

The two side edges of a piece of fabric are called the selvedges. To keep them straight, don't let the weft protrude beyond the edge of the weaving in a loop (as shown). Don't pull it in too tightly either, as this will draw in your weaving, making it narrow and uneven.

INTERLOCKING THREADS AT THE SELVEDGE

When you weave with more than one type of weft yarn and therefore more than one shuttle, you need to carry the spare weft thread up the sides of your weaving. To do this you inter-lock the different yarns by passing the shuttles around each other at the selvedge (edge) as you weave. Keep the selvedge straight by avoiding either making loops at the edges or pulling in the weft threads too tightly.

Tip When weaving with more than one shuttle rest the shuttle carrying the extra weft yarn on the table beside the loom as you weave.

JOINING IN A NEW WEFT THREAD

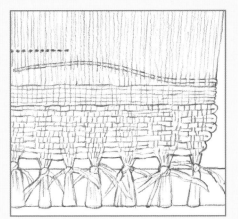

Avoid knots in the weft by over-lapping the old and the new weft ends by at least 2 in (5 cm) in the shed. Beat gently into position. These joins soon become invisible and are held firmly in place by the rows of weaving on either side.

MENDING A BROKEN WARP

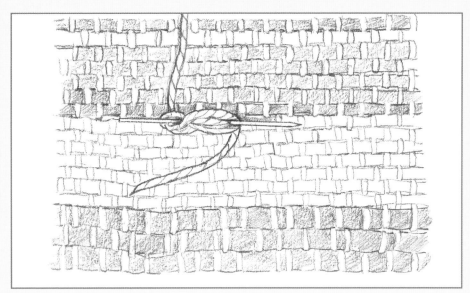

A warp may break because a thread has worn thin and snapped, or a knot has gone unnoticed and got caught in the heddle. To mend the warp place the heddle in the rest position.

Take a piece of matching thread approximately the length of your remaining warp. This will replace the remaining broken warp end wound around the back roller. Remove the broken warp end from the heddle and thread the new warp end through in its place.

Now place a straight pin into the woven fabric in line with the new thread and about 1 in (2.5 cm) back from the last woven row. Wrap the new thread around the pin in a figure eight.

Tie the new and broken warp ends in a bow near the back of the loom matching the tension to the rest of the warp.

Continue weaving and rolling forward as before. When the bow gets close to the heddle undo the bow and re-tie as before near the back roller.

When you have finished weaving and removed your fabric from the loom, remove the pin. Darn in the loose ends, then trim them close to the fabric. This will give you a secure and invisible mend.

Embellishments

These decorative touches will turn a simple piece of weaving into something special and unique.

WARP FINISHES

If you want to use the warp ends as a fringe, don't cut the weaving from the loom. Instead, untie the warp knots on the front and back rollers. Unpick the header from the start of your weaving before finishing the warp ends with one of the following techniques.

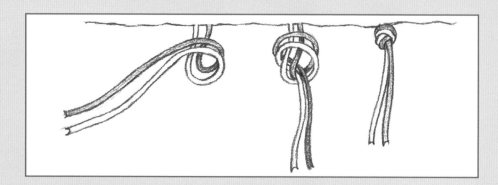

Overhand knots

Take two or three strands of warp, depending on how large you want the knot to be. Make a simple overhand knot and pull it gently up to the edge of the weaving. Repeat across the width of the warp.

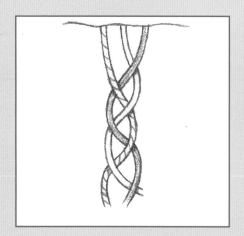

Plait

Take three strands of warp and plait them in the conventional way by passing each outside strand over the central one in turn. Make an overhand knot at the bottom of each plait.

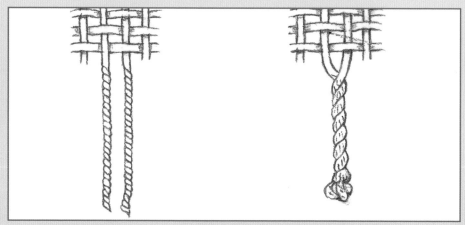

Twisted fringe

Twist each pair of warp ends towards the right (above left) until they start to crinkle up. Then pair up the warp ends and twist them towards the left (above right). Make a knot as close as possible to the bottom of each twist.

WEAVING WITH UNSPUN FIBERS

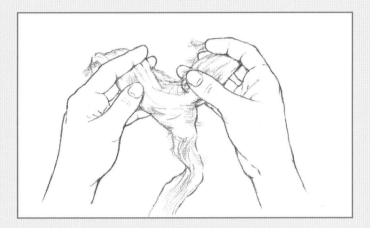

You can use unspun fibers to create exciting, tactile fabrics. Clean locks of natural or dyed fleece can be woven in by hand, overlapping the ends to create a dense but soft fabric. They can also be knotted onto the warp, giving a tufted and robust texture (see Cottage garden project, pages 104–105). You will need a well-spaced warp – dent size 5 dpi (20/10 cm) – to allow room for the fibers to fluff out.

Try using ready-prepared rovings (also called slivers) – wool locks that have been cleaned and combed to make a continuous strand – which come in a range of glorious colors. Before weaving or knotting with rovings, prepare the unspun fibers by first splitting each roving into several lengths (as shown). When weaving, you will need to beat firmly between the rows to make a robust and strong fabric.

GHIORDES (TURKISH) KNOTS

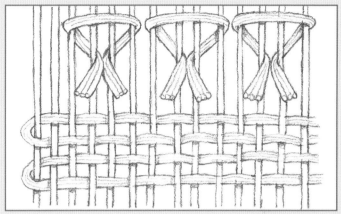

Loop a length of weft yarn across four warp ends, then draw the ends of the weft back up between the two inner warp ends. Continue making these knots across the width of the warp to create an entire row, then pull them along the warp so they sit next to the edge of your weaving. Stabilize them by weaving four or six rows of plain weave before creating the next row of ghiordes knots. Use a soft wool or cotton thread as the plain weave weft between the rows of ghiordes knots.

 Tip Both weaving with unspun fibers and making ghiordes knots use up large amounts of fiber or yarn, so have plenty on hand.

FLOAT PATTERNS

Float patterns – where the warp or weft threads 'float' over the background weaving – create exciting and complex-looking fabrics with very little effort. To make float patterns you use a pick-up stick as you weave – a flat piece of wood that is about 1 inch (2.5 cm) wide and slightly longer than the width of your weft. You can produce many different float patterns, as you can alter the stick's position as often as you choose. If the weft is more noticeable, the fabric is called 'weft-faced'. If the warp is more noticeable, then it is 'warp-faced'.

pick-up stick

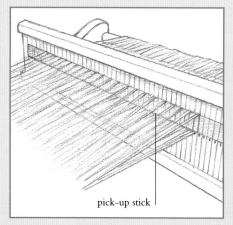

pick-up stick

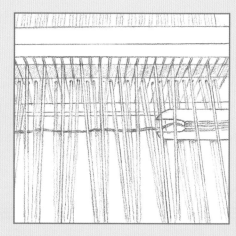

1 Put the heddle into the down position and weave in the pick-up stick between the heddle and the back roller picking up every other thread in the upper row of warp ends only. Push it to the back of the loom.

2 When the float pattern is needed, put the heddle in the rest position so there is no shed. Bring the pick-up stick forward and place it near the heddle, and turn the stick on its side. This will create a 'mini' shed between the warp ends threaded through the holes of the reed and those warp ends that are threaded through the slots of the reed and sit above the pick-up stick.

3 Pass the shuttle through the 'mini' shed. The raised warp ends will float across the plain weave. Flatten the pick-up stick and push it to the back of the loom again. Continue weaving as normal until you next need to create a float pattern.

Other types of weaving

Most of the weaving projects in this book use the rigid heddle loom and plain (tabby) weaving. There are a couple, however, that are created using card loom weaving and peg loom weaving, as described here.

CARD LOOM WEAVING

A simple loom made from stiff cardboard is useful for experimenting with unusual yarns and different textures. It is also a great alternative for making small projects.

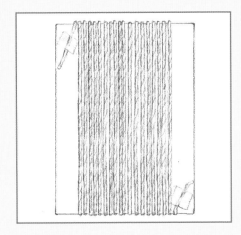

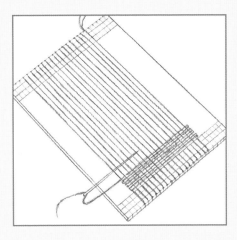

1 Choose a piece of stiff card that is a suitable size for your project. Then, starting at one edge of the card, wind a continuous warp around the front and back of the card, keeping the spacing even and the tension firm but not tight. Secure the beginning and the end of the warp with tape onto the back of the card loom.

2 Weave the weft with either your fingers or a large-eyed, blunt-ended wool needle. Push the weft down with your fingers after you weave each row.

Once you have woven the length of the card turn the card over and cut the warp along the center. Remove the weaving carefully from the card and knot the warp ends to secure the weaving. The unwoven warp ends can be cut off or used to make a fringe (see page 22).

Tip Card loom weaving is a way to experiment with other materials such as paper, plastic, grasses and twigs (see Tutti-frutti, pages 86–87).

PEG LOOM WEAVING

Peg looms are simple to use and quick to thread up. You can choose from several different sizes and densities, depending on what you want to weave. The warp yarn needs to be strong and smooth, but the weft can be made from a variety of yarns or fabric strips, including rags, fleece and strips from plastic bags. This makes them ideal for projects using recycled materials.

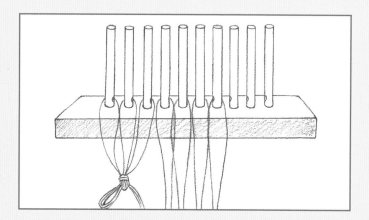

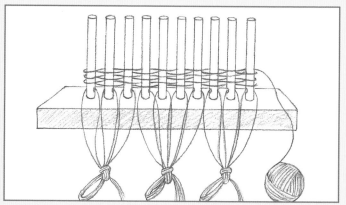

1 Clamp your peg loom firmly to the edge of a table. Cut a warp end for each peg – each warp end should be at least twice the required finished length of the project plus an extra allowance for finishing and fringeing. Lift each peg individually out of its hole and thread the warp end through its threading hole – located near the base of the peg – so that the warp length is folded in half. Once you have threaded each hole lay out the warp ends on the table, keeping them smooth and untangled. Tie the ends furthest from the pegs into small groups to prevent your weaving from falling off as it builds up and you push it along the warp. Wind your chosen weft yarn into balls.

2 Take a ball of weft and start to weave from the left, going in and out of the pegs, working from one side to the other and then around the end peg and back again. Avoid pulling the weft too tight, but keep the tension even by pressing the weft down firmly. When you join in a new ball of weft, overlap the new end over the old by at least 2 in (5 cm).

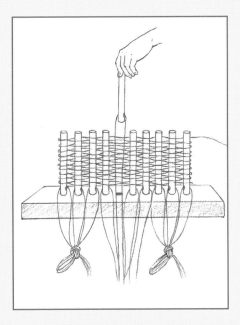

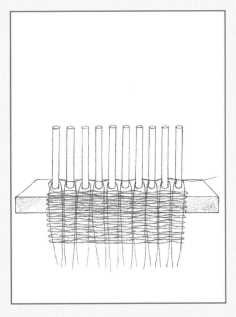

3 Weave on until you are nearly at the top of the pegs. Then, starting from the center peg, pull out each peg one at a time, easing the weaving off the peg and onto the warp.

4 Replace each of the the now empty pegs back into its hole. The top edge of the weaving should now sit near the base of the pegs. Continue weaving until the pegs are full again, then pull the pegs through your weaving and ease it onto the warp, as before. Continue this process until the entire warp is covered and your weaving complete.

5 Once all the weaving is pushed onto the warp, starting at the center, take each peg out of its hole one at a time, and pull through enough of the warp to tie in a knot. Cut the warp close to the pegs and tie the ends in bunches of four ends.

When all the pegs are removed and the warp ends knotted, adjust the weaving by pulling up the warp ends equally from either end of the fabric while pushing the weaving to the center. Finish the warp off neatly at both ends (see Warp finishes, pages 22 and 23).

 Each time you pull the pegs through the weaving, be careful not to catch the weft ends when replacing the peg in its hole.

red

Red is the color of heat,
fire, passion and love

Chilli pepper   **Cherry blossom**   **Pomegranate**   **Geranium**

Mixing a range of reds and pinks brings a far greater richness and depth of color to your weaving – and the colors don't clash once they're mixed in. This gives you the chance to use up odd balls of yarn of similar shades to create vibrant, unusual fabric. Try a pink warp with a red weft.

Equipment Rigid heddle loom. 5 shuttles

Reed 10 dpi (40/10 cm)

Warp Mixed yarns in cottons, silks and synthetics in reds and pinks
4–ply yarns: 17 wraps per in (7 wraps per cm)
DK yarns: 15 wraps per in (6 wraps per cm)

Weft Mixed yarns in cottons, wools and silks in reds and pinks. Thick and thin yarns work well together

Threading 1 end in every hole and slot

Weaving Plain weave. Use yarns randomly. Carry loose threads up the sides of the weaving, interlocking as you weave

Special feature Uses small amounts of lots of similar colors to create vibrancy

chilli pepper

Tip Follow thick threads with thin to create a balanced weave.

A vibrant mix of red and pink yarns creates an exotic flavor of hot spiciness.

Weft
Red and pink cotton, wool and silk

Warp
Red and pink cotton, silk, wool and synthetic yarn

cherry blossom

The slightest shimmer of silk can lift even the plainest of cottons to more exotic levels. This project is the perfect opportunity to use an expensive thread you might have been saving for a rainy day, mixing it in among more economical ones. You'll find that the fancier threads add a lovely drape and shimmer to the end result. For a suggestion on how to use this fabric, see the Gallery, page 108.

Equipment Rigid heddle loom. 4 shuttles

Reed 10 dpi (40/10 cm)

Warp 4-ply cotton yarns in peach, light pink, dark pink:
17 wraps per in (7 wraps per cm)
DK cotton yarn in pink: 15 wraps per in (6 wraps per cm)

Weft 4-ply cotton yarns in peach, light pink, dark pink:
17 wraps per in (7 wraps per cm)
DK cotton yarn in pink: 15 wraps per in (6 wraps per cm)
Random-dyed silk yarn: 15 wraps per in (6 wraps per cm)

Threading 1 end in every hole and slot. Random arrangement of colors

Weaving Plain weave. Use 4 shuttles at random to avoid regular stripes

Special feature Mixture of expensive and cheaper yarns

Subtle pinks of varying shades merge and meld to produce a cherry blossom confection.

Weft
Peach, light pink and dark pink cotton and silk

Warp
Peach, light pink and dark pink cotton

pomegranate

Natural hemp fiber in soft tones reflects the simple check of this fabric, created with random threading in three colors; a simple weave pattern that gives the impression of a check design without you actually having to count all the threads. It is easy to set up and weave, using organic hemp that makes a soft, pliable yarn. Use this firm fabric to make smart table mats and runners.

Equipment Rigid heddle loom. 3 shuttles

Reed 10 dpi (40/10 cm)

Warp 4-ply hemp yarn in deep pink, black and natural: 17 wraps per in (7 wraps per cm)

Weft 4-ply hemp yarn in deep pink, black and natural: 17 wraps per in (7 wraps per cm)

Threading 1 end in every hole and slot. Random threading in varied width stripes of pink, black and natural

Weaving Random stripes of pink, black and natural will build into clear check patterns as the weft crosses the warp

Special feature A 'cheat' check, very simple to achieve

 Tip Like linen, hemp yarn has very little stretch, so keep warp tension very even when winding it onto the loom. Re-tension as you weave.

The trio of colors harmonize perfectly, reminding us of the flesh and seeds of succulent pomegranates.

Weft
Deep pink, black and natural hemp

Warp
Deep pink, black and natural hemp

geranium

This brilliant red weave, with a simple but clever border of jewel-like colors that seem scattered like confetti, makes a wonderful bright wrap or throw. Sparks of iridescent color, like fireworks, created by the use of bright, random-dyed yarn, lift the intense red of the background. Add a flamboyant twisted fringe to finish (see page 21). For suggestions on how to use this fabric, see the Gallery, page 108.

Tip Try out a twisted fringe to add the finishing touch to this project.

Equipment Rigid heddle loom. 3 shuttles

Reed 7.5 dpi (30/10 cm)

Warp Soft-spun DK red wool yarn:
14 wraps per in (6 wraps per cm)
Chunky tweed red-black wool yarn:
10 wraps per in (4 wraps per cm)
Random DK wool in bright colors:
14 wraps per in (6 wraps per cm)

Weft Soft-spun DK red wool yarn:
14 wraps per in (6 wraps per cm)
Chunky tweed red-black wool yarn:
10 wraps per in (4 wraps per cm)
Random DK wool in bright colors:
14 wraps per in (6 wraps per cm)

Threading 1 end in every hole and slot. Plain border, random stripes, plain center

Weaving In same order as the weft. Plain border, random stripes, plain center. Carry spare yarns up the selvedge in the border

Special feature Simple border design with a twisted fringe

All things festive and fun are conjured up in the bright reds and scattered points of color in this exuberant weave.

Weft
Red or brightly colored and multi-colored wool and tweed wools

Warp
Red or brightly colored and multi-colored wool and tweed wools

orange

Orange is mellow and mouth-watering,
reminding us of richness and ripening

Tropical fruits   **Spice**   **Autumn**

This robust fabric is made from thick rug wool in the warp. This wool comes in a wide range of lively colors – you only need small amounts of around six shades. Thread in random, contrasting, stripes and weave yourself a strong material, ideal for making a hardwearing beach bag, to which you can add a lining or leave as it is.

Equipment Rigid heddle loom. 1 shuttle

Reed 7.5 dpi (30/10 cm)

Warp Cream, gold, blue, red, yellow and green chunky wool rug yarn:
7 wraps per in (3 wraps per cm)

Weft Rust-grey tweed 4-ply wool yarn:
17 wraps per in (7 wraps per cm)

Threading 1 end in every hole and slot. Random colors

Weaving Plain weave. Weft used double throughout

Special feature Random stripe, easy to set up with small amounts of 6 colors

Tip Beat firmly with the heddle to produce a tightly woven texture.

tropical fruits

Lively colors create a multitude of bold stripes reminiscent of tropical days.

Weft
Rust-grey tweed 4-ply wool

Warp
Cream, gold, blue, red, yellow
and green chunky wool

spice

This is a great project for using up dressmaking scraps or recycling fabric from favorite old dresses that you love too much to throw away (in this case a tablecloth). You simply cut the strips on the bias and weave them quickly into a robust piece of cloth, which you can then convert into a hard-wearing bag, mat or rug. Striped or checked fabric in strong colors works best. Avoid small patterns, flowers and pale colors – they will look too washed out.

Tip Beat firmly with the heddle to produce a firm and even weave.

Equipment Rigid heddle loom. 1 shuttle

Reed 5 dpi (20/10 cm)

Warp 4-ply orange cotton yarn: 16 wraps per in (7 wraps per cm)

Weft Checked cotton scraps cut into 1-in (2.5-cm) continuous strips, cut on the bias

Threading 1 end in every hole and slot

Weaving Plain weave

Special feature Recycled cheesecloth cotton fabric cut from an old tablecloth

Checked cotton fabric in vibrant oranges, blues, greens and yellows conveys heat, exotic aromas and rich hues.

Weft
Multi-coloured, bias-cut
cotton fabric

Warp
Orange cotton yarn

Bouclé yarn, with its tight and exotic loops, gives a tweedy and bubbly appearance to plain weave. Bright accent yarns in both warp and weft give a subtle zip to the resulting fabric. Leave the accent yarn hanging loose on either side as you weave, to create additional interest. A subtle check design appears among the loopy bouclé and shiny accent yarn.

autumn

Equipment Rigid heddle loom. 5 shuttles

Reed 10 dpi (40/10 cm)

Warp Orange 4-ply wool yarn:
17 wraps per in (7 wraps per cm)
Orange-black-yellow accent yarn:
15 wraps per in (6 wraps per cm)

Weft Orange bouclé yarn, wool and acrylic: 12 wraps per in (5 wraps per cm)
Orange-black-yellow accent yarn:
15 wraps per in (6 wraps per cm)

Threading 1 end in every hole and slot. 2 accent yarns and 8 wool yarns, repeated across width

Weaving Plain weave with bouclé and accent yarn

Special feature Subtle check design using bouclé and shiny accent yarn

Unwoven bouclé looks playful and fun and gives woven fabric a soft, tweedy look.

Weft
Orange bouclé and orange-black-yellow accent yarn

Warp
Orange wool and orange-black-yellow accent yarn

yellow

Yellow is full of hope,
promise, joy and light

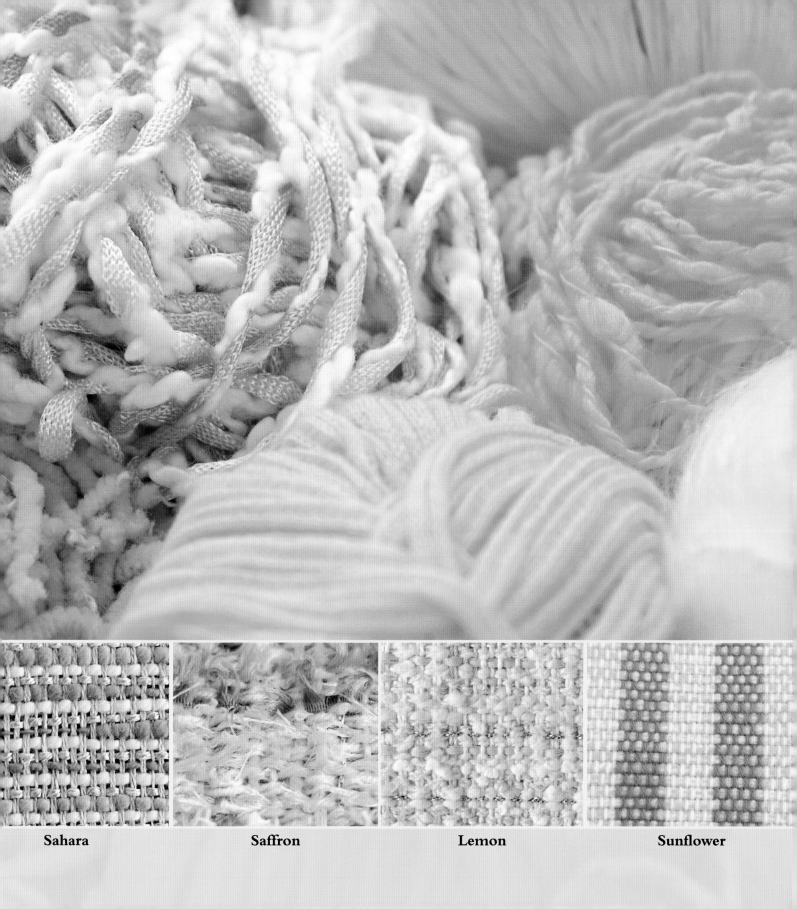

Sahara

Saffron

Lemon

Sunflower

sahara

Natural linen warp supports the silk, cotton and slub yarns for this classic, elegant weave, creating a ribbed fabric in which the warp is threaded double. Try the natural linen with other colorways, such as pinks and oranges, for a different look. For a suggestion on how to use this fabric, see the Gallery, page 108.

Equipment Rigid heddle loom. 3 shuttles

Reed 10 dpi (40/10 cm)

Warp Natural fine linen yarn: 28 wraps per in
(12 wraps per cm)

Weft Brown space-dyed slub cotton: 9 wraps per in
(3 wraps per cm)
Golden yellow silk cotton mix yarn: 12 wraps per in
(4 wraps per cm)
Lemon yellow cotton yarn: (12 wraps per in)
(4 wraps per cm)

Threading 2 linen threads in every slot and every hole

Weaving Plain weave using 1 row slub cotton, 1 row
silk cotton mix and 1 row plain cotton. Repeat

Special feature A ribbed fabric using warp threaded
double, giving an elegant appearance

 Tip Keep the tension tight and beat firmly.

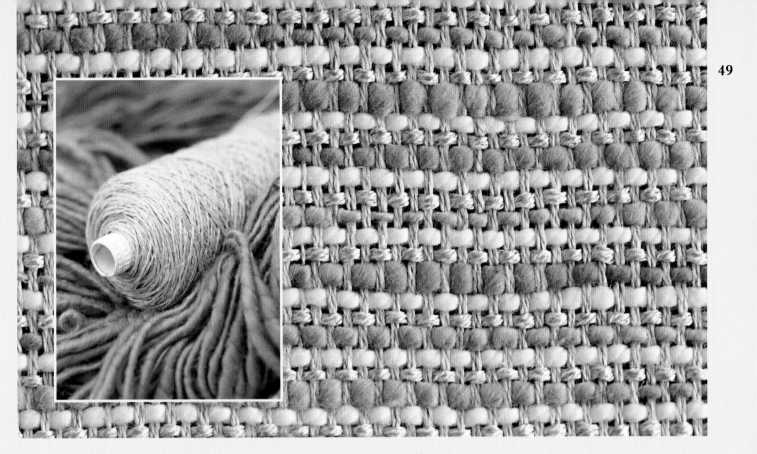

Parched desert sands and dry lands are evoked in this harmonious weave.

Weft
Brown space-dyed slub cotton,
golden yellow silk and cotton
mix, lemon yellow cotton

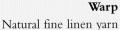

Warp
Natural fine linen yarn

For an offbeat shawl or throw that adds a little sparkle, try this brightly hued tartan effect. Mixed yarns in brilliant yellows and greens create a light but warm fabric. Add a sparkly thread for extra glamour and eyelash yarns for a fluffy texture. If you want to use up lots of different bits of yarn in related colors, this is a perfect project; you can achieve a subtle check as you go along.

saffron

Equipment Rigid heddle loom. 3 shuttles

Reed 5 dpi (20/10 cm)

Warp Mixed yarns in yellows and greens
4-ply yarns: 20 wraps per in (8 wraps per cm)
Eyelash yarn and mohair yarn:
5 wraps per in (2 wraps per cm)
Fine lurex: 35 wraps per in (15 wraps per cm)

Weft Mixed yarns in yellows and greens
4-ply yarns: 20 wraps per in (8 wraps per cm)
Eyelash yarn and mohair yarn:
5 wraps per in (2 wraps per cm)
Chunky mohair yarn:
5 wraps per in (2 wraps per cm)
Fine lurex: 35 wraps per in (15 wraps per cm)

Threading 1 end in every hole and slot.
Finer ends in holes, thicker ends in slots

Weaving Plain weave. Alternate between three shuttles. Randomly change each shuttle to avoid regular stripes, interlocking the spare threads at the edge as you weave

Special features Uses up lots of bits of related-color yarns. Achieves a subtle check

Tip Beat very lightly to create an open weave.

Soft yellow warp threads and yellow weft evoke the bright hues of exotic saffron.

Weft
Yellow and green wool, eyelash yarn, mohair, chunky mohair and fine lurex

Warp
Yellow and green wool, eyelash yarn, mohair and fine lurex

Experiment with cottons, viscose and washable raffia to produce a wonderfully flexible and easy-to-wear fabric in softly blending shades. If you want to prevent regular stripes from appearing in the finished piece, change the shuttles at frequent, random intervals.

lemon

Equipment Rigid heddle loom. 4 shuttles

Reed 10 dpi (40/10 cm

Warp Mixed cotton yarns in yellow, beige and white:
10–14 wraps per in (4–6 wraps per cm)

Weft Yellow washable raffia yarn:
10 wraps per in (3 wraps per cm)
Gold viscose ribbon yarn:
12 wraps per in (4 wraps per cm)
Yellow and white bouclé cotton yarn:
8 wraps per in (3 wraps per cm)

Threading Spaced and crammed warp. Mix the colors and yarns together and thread the reed randomly

Weaving Using all four shuttles weave one, two or three rows of each yarn, taking care to carry each yarn up the sides of the weaving, interlocking as you weave

Special feature An open sett creates a flexible fabric

 Tip Beat firmly and the spaces in the warp threading will keep the fabric soft and open-textured.

Fresh lemons and beiges team

perfectly with gold and white

to create a zesty weave.

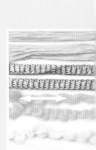

Weft
Yellow raffia, gold viscose and
yellow and white bouclé cotton

Warp
Yellow, beige and white
mixed cottons

Quick and easy to make, this lively design with a classic look took its inspiration from an Amish hand-woven mat made in Lancaster County. Clever warp and weft combinations give simple, summery color choices an intriguing folksy look. The close weave makes them thick enough to use as place settings and coasters. Weave a set of mats for yourself and then more for family and friends – they make wonderfully simple gifts. For a suggestion on how to use this fabric, see the Gallery, page 108.

sunflower

Equipment Rigid heddle loom. 1 shuttle

Reed 10 dpi (40/10 cm)

Warp Fine orange and yellow wool yarn: 25 wraps per in (10 wraps per cm) 4-ply lemon and gold wool yarn: 17 wraps per in (7 wraps per cm)

Weft 8–10 strands of yellow and lemon wools wound onto the shuttle together

Threading 1 orange and 1 gold together. 1 yellow and 1 lemon together. Half-inch (1 cm) stripes of each, threaded as a pair in each hole and each slot

Weaving Plain weave. Beat firmly

Special feature A warp-faced fabric with a grouped weft. This is a small project that is quick to weave

Tip Multi-strand weft is great for using up leftover yarns; try weaving each mat with a different combination of colors.

Plain stripes in summer colors are reminiscent of a simple, outdoor way of life and good living.

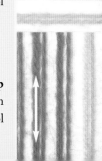

Weft
Lemon and yellow wool

Warp
Orange and yellow, and lemon
and gold wool

green

Fresh and crisp, green is full of nature's goodness

Grasslands   **Waterweed**   **Pine forest**

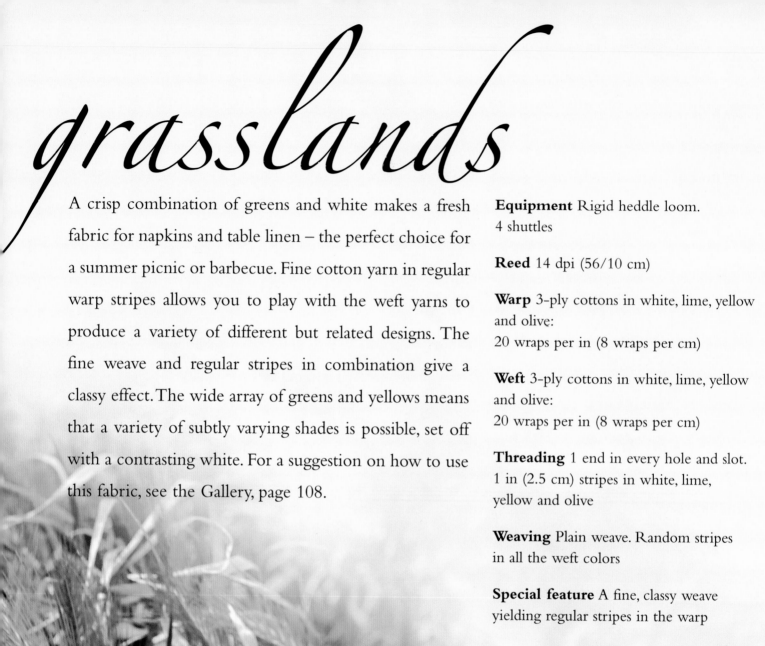

grasslands

A crisp combination of greens and white makes a fresh fabric for napkins and table linen – the perfect choice for a summer picnic or barbecue. Fine cotton yarn in regular warp stripes allows you to play with the weft yarns to produce a variety of different but related designs. The fine weave and regular stripes in combination give a classy effect. The wide array of greens and yellows means that a variety of subtly varying shades is possible, set off with a contrasting white. For a suggestion on how to use this fabric, see the Gallery, page 108.

Equipment Rigid heddle loom. 4 shuttles

Reed 14 dpi (56/10 cm)

Warp 3-ply cottons in white, lime, yellow and olive: 20 wraps per in (8 wraps per cm)

Weft 3-ply cottons in white, lime, yellow and olive: 20 wraps per in (8 wraps per cm)

Threading 1 end in every hole and slot. 1 in (2.5 cm) stripes in white, lime, yellow and olive

Weaving Plain weave. Random stripes in all the weft colors

Special feature A fine, classy weave yielding regular stripes in the warp

Tip Beat firmly and keep the tension even.

Give yourself a year-long reminder of long, hot summer days with these fresh greens in grassy hues.

Weft
Yellow, lime, olive and white cotton

Warp
White, lime, yellow, and olive cotton

waterweed

Eyelash yarn, soft and iridescent, combines well with a smooth, fine wool to produce an intriguing fabric, perfect for casual scarves, bags or waistcoats. The loose weave makes this a quick and easy project and the end result is quirky and original.

Tip Beat very gently to let the yarn fluff up.

Equipment Rigid heddle loom. 1 shuttle

Reed 10 dpi (40/10 cm)

Warp Green fine wool yarn:
15 wraps per in (5 wraps per cm)
Green and blue eyelash or fringe yarn:
8 wraps per in (3 wraps per cm)

Weft Green and blue eyelash yarn:
8 wraps per in (3 wraps per cm)

Threading Fine wool yarn every hole.
Eyelash yarn every slot

Weaving Plain weave

Special feature An unusual effect that is quick and easy to weave

Add an exotic touch to your evening wardrobe with this glistening eyelash yarn and fine wool combination.

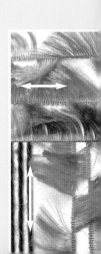

Weft
Green and blue eyelash yarn

Warp
Green wool and green and blue eyelash yarn

pine forest

Hard-wearing jute fiber produces a sturdy fabric, ideal for making a bag for carrying heavy books and shopping. Use ordinary garden twine in a variety of colors to add contrast and accentuate the pattern. Cut the floats after the fabric is finished to add eye-catching detail. Sew in a tough calico lining for additional strength and long life.

Equipment Rigid heddle loom. 2 shuttles. 1 pick-up stick

Reed 5 dpi (20/10 cm)

Warp Natural jute thread: 12 wraps per in (5 wraps per cm)

Weft Natural jute thread and green garden twine: 12 wraps per in (5 wraps per cm)

Threading 1 end in every hole and slot

Weaving Plain weave, 3 in (8 cm) with natural jute thread. Beat firmly. With the heddle in the down position, thread the pick-up stick through the raised warps, across 4 threads and under 5 threads. Repeat across the warp.

   For pattern weaving, pull the pick-up stick close to the back of the heddle. For plain weave push it to the back of the loom (see page 23). Alternate rows of plain weave in natural jute with pattern weave in green twine, wrapping the shuttles at the side to prevent unravelling for 2 in (5 cm)

Special features Weft floats. Hardwearing jute and twine

Tip Check the tension regularly to keep the weaving even.

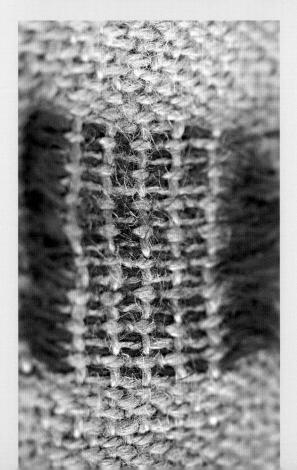

Green floats contrast effectively with the natural jute, evoking pine needles and forests.

Weft
Natural jute and green
garden twine

Warp
Natural jute

blue

Blue is the color of our dreams,
our moods and our inner soul

Sea　　　　　**Rainbow**　　　　　**Midnight**　　　　　**Peacock**

sea

The softness of handspun singles yarn for both warp and weft gives this fabric a wonderful drape and handle. Random dyeing in the fleece allows the colors to mingle freely throughout the yarn. Any softly spun wool, such as the Shetland yarns used here, will give a similar feel and look. Use the woven length to make a warm, enfolding shawl or a wonderfully luxurious throw.

Equipment Rigid heddle loom. 1 shuttle

Reed 10 dpi (40/10 cm)

Warp Woollen yarn in blue/green mixture: 12 wraps per in (5 wraps per cm)

Weft Woollen yarn in a blue/white mixture: 12 wraps per in (5 wraps per cm)

Threading 1 end in every hole and slot

Weaving Plain weave

Special feature Soft, tweedy effect

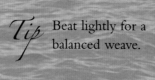

Tip Beat lightly for a balanced weave.

Subtle shades of blue

with strong shades of green

capture the hidden depths

of the sea.

Weft
Blue/white mixture wool

Warp
Blue/green mixture wool

Think of a rainbow arching suddenly across a stormy sky – thick singles in random-dyed colors float across a dark blue background. This weave gets its striking effect with floating warps, achieved by using a pick-up stick (see page 23). It makes a good strong fabric suitable for soft furnishings and cushion covers. Experiment with other color combinations for lots of other imaginative results. Play around with the patterns by using a pick-up stick behind the heddle. Pick up as many or as few warp threads as you want and watch the pattern develop as you weave.

Equipment Rigid heddle loom. 1 shuttle. 1 pick-up stick

Reed 5 dpi (20/10 cm)

Warp Blue alpaca wool yarn:
13 wraps per in (3 wraps per cm)
Rainbow slub yarn:
7 wraps per in (2 wraps per cm)

Weft Dark blue chunky or sport wool yarn:
8 wraps per in (2 wraps per cm)

Threading 4 ends of alpaca. 1 end slub yarn. Repeat across the heddle

Weaving Plain weave, beating firmly to cover warp threads

Special feature Warp-faced floats

rainbow

Tip Insert a pick-up stick behind the heddle and under all the rainbow slub yarn threads. Weave 5 rows with the pick-up stick in the raised position, only weaving over the blue alpaca wool warp. For the sixth row lower the pick-up stick and weave over all the warp threads, making sure you anchor down the slub yarn as you weave. Repeat.

Dark shades blend with the deep blue background, while bright colors burst onto the surface.

Weft
Dark blue chunky wool

Warp
Blue alpaca and rainbow slub

midnight

Equipment Rigid heddle loom.
2 shuttles

Reed 10 dpi (40/10 cm)

Warp 4-ply wool and silk yarn in blue
and grey:
17 wraps per in (7 wraps per cm)
Mohair, two-toned blue-gold yarn:
8 wraps per in (3 wraps per cm)

Weft 4-ply wool and silk yarn in blue:
17 wraps per in (7 wraps per cm)
Mohair, two-toned blue-gold yarn:
8 wraps per in (3 wraps per cm)

Threading 4 mohair, miss a hole and
slot, 6 wool/silk mix, miss a hole and a
slot. Repeat across width

Weaving Plain weave. 4 rows mohair.
3 rows blue wool/silk. Repeat

Special feature Open-spaced warp
allowing soft drape

The open-weave effect of this spaced warp gives a
marvellous soft feel, highly suitable for a loosely draped
scarf or shawl. You can experiment with a variety of soft
mohair yarns, in contrasting light and dark tones. In this
project, inky blue and grey two-toned mohair contrasts
with plain light blue and white. For a suggestion on how
to use this fabric, see the Gallery, page 108.

Tip Beat gently with the heddle to
produce a light open texture.

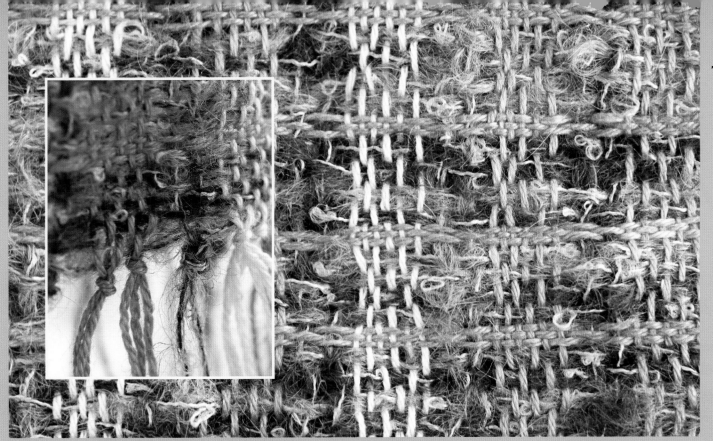

For a romantic evening shawl, a combination of dark mohair and light wool evokes the clear night sky.

Weft
Blue wool/silk and
blue-gold mohair

Warp
Blue and grey wool/silk and
blue-gold mohair

peacock

Rainbow-dyed yarns create a kaleidoscope of color all by themselves – in this example there is an extensive range – from deep turquoise blue through dark magentas and purples, fading to mustard yellows. Choose a toning yarn for the warp to support rather than detract from the colors in the weft. Using rainbow-dyed yarn, your finished piece of weaving will be full of color surprises.

Equipment Rigid heddle loom. 1 shuttle

Reed 5 dpi (20/10 cm)

Warp 4-ply alpaca wool yarn: 15 wraps per in (6 wraps per cm)
Rainbow-dyed slub wool yarn: 6 wraps per in (2 wraps per cm)

Weft Rainbow-dyed slub wool yarn:
6 wraps per in (2 wraps per cm)

Threading 1 end in every hole and slot. 4 thin yarns, 1 thick. Repeat, ending with 4 thin yarns

Weaving Plain weave, slub yarn only. Beat lightly

Special feature Slub yarn used in both the warp and the weft

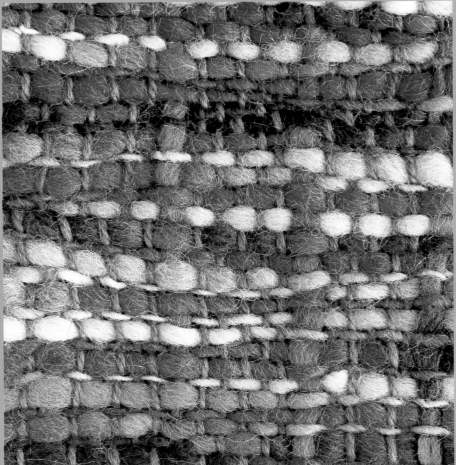

Vibrant turquoises, magentas and yellows in random order remind us of the glorious plumage of the peacock.

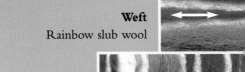

Weft
Rainbow slub wool

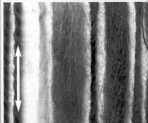

Warp
Blue alpaca wool and rainbow slub wool

purple

Mystery and magic
abound in this exotic color

Pansy   **Heather**   **Amethyst**   **Lavender**

Add a little shimmer and shine to your weaving with brilliant rainbow ribbon yarn. Many people assume that these yarns are too difficult to work with, but using a plain cotton yarn between the rows helps to stabilize the slippery fancy thread and also makes it go further.

pansy

Equipment Rigid heddle loom. 2 shuttles

Reed 10 dpi (40/10 cm)

Warp Variegated pink cotton yarn:
16 wraps per in (7 wraps per cm)

Weft Rainbow ribbon yarn:
8 wraps per in (3 wraps per cm)
Purple mercerized cotton yarn:
16 wraps per in (6 wraps per cm)

Threading 1 in every hole and slot

Weaving Plain weave. 1 row ribbon yarn,
2 rows cotton yarn

Special feature Ribbon weft

Tip Beat gently to avoid squashing the ribbon yarn used for the weft.

Clever combinations of pinks, purples and shiny yellow bring to mind beds of pansies.

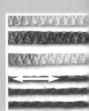

Weft
Rainbow ribbon yarn and
purple mercerized cotton

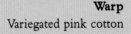

Warp
Variegated pink cotton

heather

A fine linen thread used double in both the warp and weft gives you the chance to play with the subtleties of shading by simply changing just one of the colored threads in the weft as you weave. The resulting fabric is both delicate and crisp, making it a perfect fabric for mats and runners.

Equipment Rigid heddle loom. 1 shuttle

Reed 12 or 15 dpi (48/10 cm or 60 per 10 cm)

Warp Fine purple linen thread used double: 40 wraps per in (12 wraps per cm)

Weft Fine purple, mauve and grey linen thread used double: 40 wraps per in (12 wraps per cm)

Threading 1 double end in every hole and slot. Use double throughout

Weaving Hopsack weave when the yarn is used double for warp and weft

Special feature Hopsack weave, toning shades

Tip Keep the linen warp as tight as possible. Use the heddle to beat firmly after the shuttle has been passed through the shed and after changing sheds.

Like the tones of a blanket of heather, the slight change of thread color creates a subtle change of pace and shading.

Weft
Purple, mauve and grey linen thread

Warp
Purple linen thread

A softly spun, thick woollen yarn forms a perfect background for a smooth, shiny ribbon yarn, creating an elegant modern fabric with a regular pattern – ideal for an informal unstructured jacket, or a cosy wrap or scarf.

amethyst

Equipment Rigid heddle loom. 2 shuttles

Reed 5 dpi (20/10 cm)

Warp Chunky lilac woollen yarn:
10 wraps per in (4 wraps per cm)
Lilac viscose ribbon yarn:
12 wraps per in (5 wraps per cm)

Weft Chunky lilac woollen yarn:
10 wraps per in (4 wraps per cm)
Lilac viscose ribbon yarn:
12 wraps per in (5 wraps per cm)

Threading 1 ribbon yarn in every hole.
1 chunky yarn in every slot

Weaving Plain weave using alternate shuttles to match the warp threading

Special feature Soft wool background for shiny ribbon yarn

Tip Beat gently to produce a balanced weave.

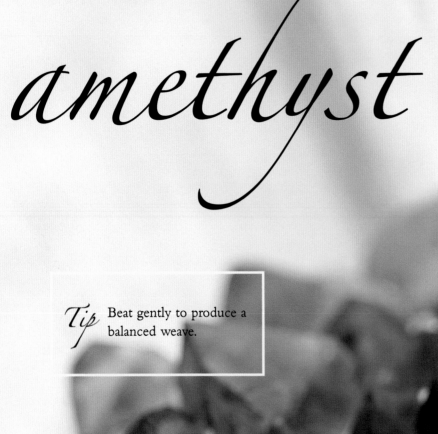

The shiny ribbon yarn catches the light in this soft weave — like the glinting facets of an amethyst crystal.

Weft
Chunky lilac wool and lilac viscose ribbon yarn

Warp
Chunky lilac wool and lilac viscose ribbon yarn

lavender

A simple self-check is created using a space-dyed yarn in shades of violet, mauve and purple in both the warp and the weft, reminding us of rolling hills and upland blooms. Add extra purple warp threads to enhance the color balance of violets, mauves and purples and weave enough fabric to make an easy lightweight spring jacket or summer top.

Equipment Rigid heddle loom. 1 shuttle

Reed 10 dpi (40/10 cm)

Warp Space-dyed chunky acrylic yarn in purple shades:
7 wraps per in (3 wraps per cm)
DK purple acrylic: 15 wraps per in (6 wraps per cm)

Weft Space-dyed chunky acrylic yarn in purple shades

Threading DK in the holes. Chunky yarn in the slots.
1 thread end in every hole and slot

Weaving Plain weave. Beat lightly

Special feature Soft check pattern using space-dyed yarn

Tip Handwash and air dry for a soft but firm fabric. Neaten edges after cutting.

Space-dyed yarn creates random shadings of lighter and darker mauves and purples like lavender fields.

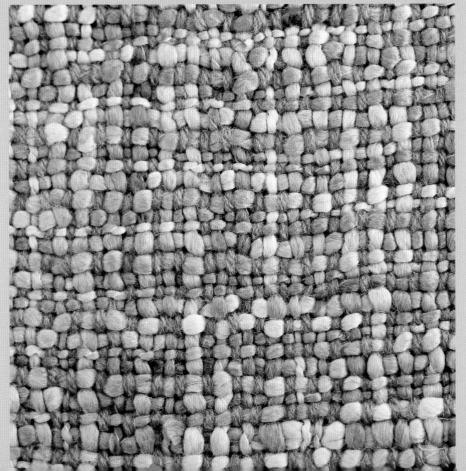

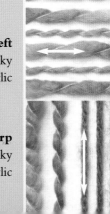

Weft
Purple space-dyed chunky
acrylic

Warp
Purple space-dyed chunky
acrylic and DK purple acrylic

recycled

Things you might think of throwing away have endless weaving possibilities

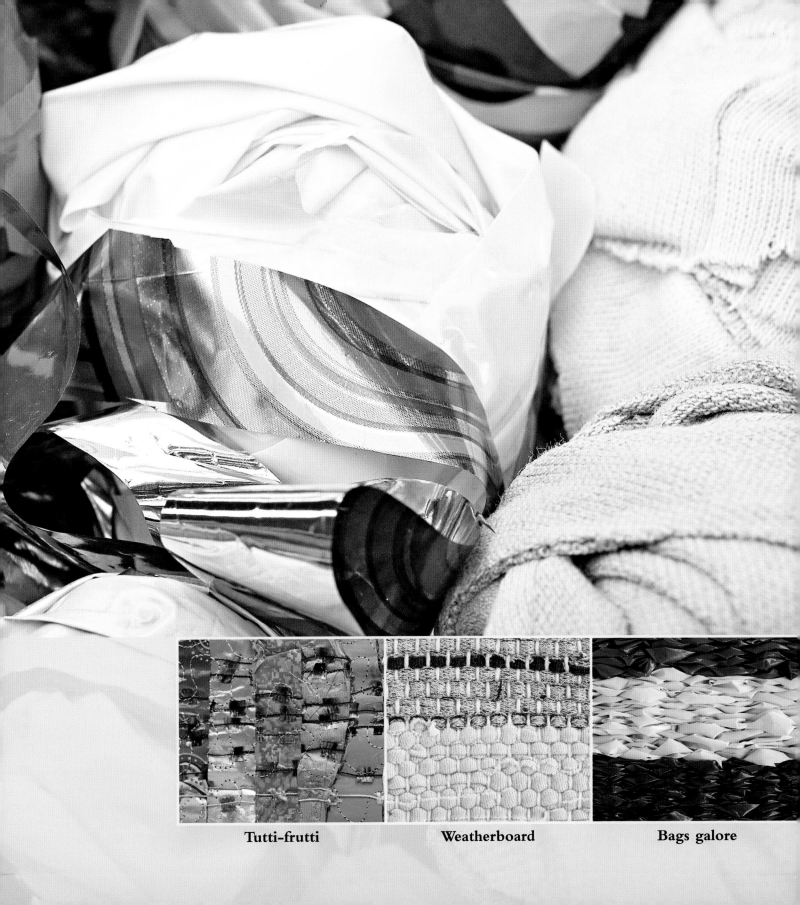

Tutti-frutti   **Weatherboard**   **Bags galore**

Save up all that lovely wrapping paper and cellophane and those brightly colored plastic bags and ribbons that are too nice to throw away but not smooth enough to reuse. Cut it all up into wide strips and weave through with your fingers using a fixed frame rather than a loom. You can make highly original gift items, such as notebooks and folders, in no time at all. For a suggestion on how to use this fabric, see the Gallery, page 109.

tutti-frutti

Equipment Card loom frame made of stiff cardboard (see page 22)

Reed Not applicable

Warp Any fancy yarn

Weft Wrapping paper, cellophane, tissue paper, plastic bags, ribbon and colored string

Threading Wind the warp firmly around the frame, securing it with a knot at the beginning and end

Weaving Cut the papers and plastic into wide strips the width of the frame. Weave each piece through the warp, leaving the edges loose until the frame is filled

Special feature Simple frame and papers

Tip Before cutting the weaving from the frame, iron a strip of fusible webbing to the back to secure all the threads. Then cut off the weaving and mount it onto a backing fabric.

Weave enough to cover your notebooks or cut up to make personalized gift tags and greetings cards.

Weft
Paper, cellophane, tissue paper, plastic bags, ribbon and string

Warp
Fancy yarn

This project uses up a pile of old T-shirts destined for the recycling bin or charity shop – all in harmonious blues and greys. Since all are thoroughly worn and well-washed, they won't let you down by shrinking or fading, but will bring you happy, lasting holiday memories. The warp in cream cotton provides a crisp contrast and professional touch when it is used to make the borders and fringes. For suggestions on how to use this fabric, see the Gallery, page 109.

Equipment Rigid heddle loom

Reed 5 dpi (20/10 cm)

Warp White DK craft cotton:
15 wraps per in (6 wraps per cm)

Weft Assorted blue fabrics cut into ½ in (1 cm) strips. Sweaters, socks, T-shirts and stretch fabrics are ideal as they do not fray

Threading 1 end in every hole and slot

Weaving Random strips in blue

Special feature Uses an assortment of similar-coloured garments cut into rags for recycling

 Tip Avoid stretching the weft as it will pull in the sides. To join a new color, taper the ends when overlapping to make an invisible join.

weatherboard

Reminders of open expanses of sea and sky are woven into this rugged fabric, highly suitable for mats and rugs.

Weft
Blue jersey fabric strips

Warp
White DK craft cotton

Plastic bags just seem to multiply all by themselves. Recycle some of the hundreds you may be hoarding and make a quick, hard-wearing doormat or a nice, thick surface for your pet to lie on. If you tend to accumulate special bags from holidays, days out, feasts and festivals, use them to make a permanent memento of good times, like an old patchwork quilt.

bags galore

Equipment Peg loom (see page 24)

Reed ½-in (1-cm) pegs set ½ in (1 cm) apart

Warp White DK craft cotton: 15 wraps per in (6 wraps per cm)

Weft Plastic carrier bags cut into 1 in-wide strips (2–3 cm). Starting at the open end, cut each bag in a spiral around the circumference of the bag to make a continuous length

Threading 1 double thread in every peg

Weaving Weave continuous strips of plastic. Overlap the new color strips when joining. Push the strips down so they completely cover the warp

Special features Quick to make on a peg loom. Recycled plastic bags

Tip Use similar thickness of bags and avoid biodegradables! To finish, tie the warp threads in overhand knots in clusters of four.

Select interestingly colored bags and arrange the colors to make a subtle or bold statement.

Weft
Plastic bag strips

Warp
White DK craft cotton

naturals

Explore the subtle
beauty of undyed shades

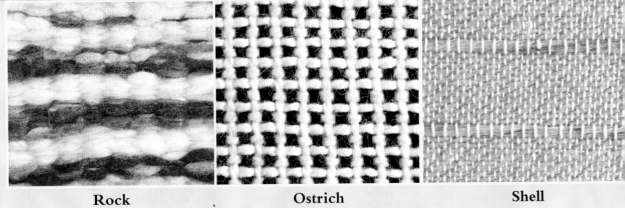

Rock   **Ostrich**   **Shell**

Natural greys, creams and browns of a Jacob fleece can be drastically different from one sheep to another and also vary with age. Why not create a lovely soft, thick mat, highly reminiscent of the original sheep? Use a simple peg loom and unspun fleece to get a really thick effect – just the thing to invite your bare feet on a cold winter's morning. For a suggestion on how to use this fabric, see the Gallery, page 109.

rock

Equipment Peg loom

Reed ½-in (1-cm) pegs set ½-in (1-cm) apart

Warp White DK craft cotton: 11 wraps per in (5 wraps per cm)

Weft Clean, unspun fleece in natural colours, teased out into locks. Use a fleece at least 6 in (15 cm) in length

Threading 1 doubled craft cotton thread per peg

Weaving Tease the locks a little to open them up. Wind them firmly in between the pegs, overlapping new locks as you weave. Push the fleece down firmly to completely hide the warp thread and make a really strong fabric

Special features Unspun fleece in natural colors. Easy to make on a peg loom (see page 24)

 Tip Uses lots of fleece – so be prepared!

Dense weaving produces a really thick, woolly effect, creating a fabric that is soft and durable underfoot.

Weft
Natural unspun fleece

Warp
White DK craft cotton

Using simple alternating black and white warp and the color and weave technique, you can create three striking fine weave patterns, each with a very different look. Experiment with different color combinations, but restrict yourself to two for each item. Sturdy black and white cotton is ideal to make this hard-wearing cloth, suitable for tea towels and other dependable domestic items. For a suggestion on how to use this fabric, see the Gallery, page 109.

ostrich

Tips Set up enough warp to weave several different color combinations. Weave strips of card in between design pieces to allow for cutting off and fringing. Machine along cut edges with a small zigzag stitch. Beat firmly.

Equipment Rigid heddle loom. 2 shuttles

Reed 14 dpi (56/10 cm)

Warp 4-ply cotton yarn in black and white: 20 wraps per in (8 wraps per cm)

Weft 4-ply cotton in black and white: 20 wraps per in (8 wraps per cm)

Threading 1 end in every hole and slot. White in holes, black in slots

Weaving 1st pattern: all white with black border. 2nd pattern: 2 rows black, 2 rows white. 3rd pattern: 3 rows black, 3 rows white Interlock weft threads at selvedge

Special feature Three patterns using the color and weave technique

Plain black and white in three different guises, produced by clever weft combinations.

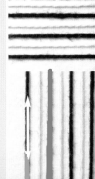

Weft
Black and white 4-ply cotton

Warp
Black and white 4-ply cotton

Natural fibers and colors work together superbly when you want to create timeless, everyday fabrics – perfect for furnishing accents such as cushions and seat covers. Cotton and linen yarns provide a hard-wearing, easily washed material, with a feature yarn adding surface interest to the smoothness of the plain weave. Try using plain threads to create a simple background for more expensive and interesting yarns. For a suggestion on how to use this fabric, see the Gallery, page 109.

Equipment Rigid heddle. 2 shuttles

Reed 10 dpi (40/10 cm)

Warp White fine cotton yarn:
20 wraps per in (8 wraps per cm)

Weft Natural linen and silk yarn:
15 wraps per in (6 wraps per cm)
Natural feature yarn:
5 wraps per in (2 wraps per cm)

Threading 1 end in every hole and slot

Weaving Plain weave with linen and silk for 6 in (15 cm). 1 row of feature yarn, followed by 2 in (5 cm) linen and silk, then 1 row of feature yarn. Repeat the above sequence, ending with 6 in (15 cm) of plain weave

Special feature Mixing linen, silk and cotton yarns together gives beautiful, natural tones

shell

 Tip Use plain threads to create a background for more expensive and interesting yarns.

Save up your best yarns to feature as surface interest in this weave. Focus on creating texture contrasts.

Weft
Natural linen and silk, and natural feature yarn

Warp
White fine cotton yarn

fun extras

Have some moments of weaving madness!

Beachcombing

Cottage garden

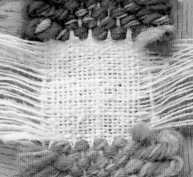

Color cubes

If you like collecting bits and pieces on beach walks, then this is the perfect project for you. Driftwood, seaweed and shells, netting and dried seaweed gathered from the shoreline are combined with natural wools, linens and silks to make an exciting and attractive way of displaying nature's wonders. Try hanging yours in front of a window to accentuate sculptural shapes. For a suggestion on how to use this fabric, see the Gallery, page 109.

beach–combing

Equipment Rigid heddle loom. 3 shuttles

Reed 10 dpi (40/10 cm)

Warp Smooth, natural-colored wool:
11 wraps per in (4 wraps per cm)

Weft Driftwood, old rope, twigs, seashells. Natural colored wool, cotton and silk yarns in small amounts:
12 wraps per in (5 wraps per cm)

Threading 1 end in every hole and slot

Weaving Plain weave. Plain weave 5 or 6 rows of wool or silk as background, then insert the driftwood under 2 or 3 warp threads, enough to anchor it down. Weave another few rows of wool or silk before adding in the next feature object. Continue until your design is complete. Knot the warp at the end of the weaving to secure all threads before hanging

Special feature Found objects form the weft

The perfect way of displaying all your beach finds — and they tone well with natural wool and cotton.

Weft
Found objects and wool, cotton and silk in natural colors

Warp
Natural-colored smooth wool

When you are choosing your fleece for this project, think of fragrant sweet peas in a gloriously colorful summer garden or framing an old cottage front door. Use the very simple but traditional technique of ghiordes knotting with unspun fleece, which produces a thick, tufted, rug-like effect. You'll be able to achieve this fun, woolly look by using chunky rainbow fleece – perfect for scatter cushions and small bedside rugs. For a suggestion on how to use this fabric, see the Gallery, page 109.

Equipment Rigid heddle loom. 1 shuttle

Reed 5 dpi (20/10 cm)

Warp White DK craft cotton:
15 wraps per in (6 wraps per cm)

Weft Chunky wool in natural:
10 wraps per in (4 wraps per cm)
Rainbow-colored sheep's fleece
approximately 4 in (10 cm) long

Threading 1 end in every hole and slot

Weaving Plain weave. 8 rows of chunky wool. 1 row of ghiordes knots using fleece or tops. Repeat

Special feature Locks of unspun fleece tied in ghiordes knots (see page 22)

Tip When making the ghiordes knots don't pull them too tight. The 8 rows of plain weave in between keep the knots in place.

cottage garden

Vibrant shades of soft fleece are evocative of country cottage gardens in summer.

Weft
Natural chunky wool and
rainbow wool fleece

Warp
White DK craft cotton

This is a fun and imaginative way to use up all your scraps of thick yarn left over from other projects. Try out a variety of color variations and see what works best. Thread colorful, coordinating beads onto the fringe and hang the finished piece from a piece of dowelling — against a wall if you want the colors on display, or in a window if you want to accentuate the shapes.

color cubes

Equipment Rigid heddle loom. 2 shuttles

Reed 10 dpi (40/10 cm)

Warp Thick, yellow linen or cotton yarn: 15 wraps per in (5 wraps per cm)

Weft Thick, yellow linen or cotton yarn: 15 wraps per in (5 wraps per cm) Chunky multi-colored wool yarns: 6 wraps per in (2 wraps per cm)

Threading Thread 20 holes and slots. Leave 20 holes and slots empty. Repeat across the heddle

Weaving Beginning with the linen, weave across the threads for 2 in (5 cm), keeping the tension across the floats. For the color blocks use the thick yarn, weaving each block individually. Repeat

Special feature Widely spaced warp creates blocks with gaps

Tip To finish, plait or knot the remaining warp threads, adding beads or other decorations.

Choose bright yarns to create vivid blocks of color — you only need small amounts.

Weft
Yellow linen and multi-colored chunky wool

Warp
Yellow linen

a gallery of weaving

Cherry blossom

A touch of shimmering pink silk makes this otherwise cotton scarf suitable for both day and evening wear. For instructions on how to weave this fabric, see page 32.

Geranium

Cosy red to warm you up on winter outings. For instructions on how to weave this fabric, see page 36.

Sahara

Linen in the warp makes this a sturdy fabric, suitable for showing off as a table runner. For instructions on how to weave this fabric, see page 48.

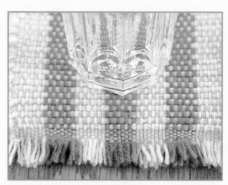

Sunflower

Multi-stranded wools create a greater thickness that is solid enough for coasters and mats. For instructions on how to weave this fabric, see page 54.

Grasslands

Fine cottons weave into an ideal fabric for making smart napkins and table linen. For instructions on how to weave this fabric, see page 58.

Midnight

Luxurious mohair lends a soft touch to this atmospheric evening stole. For instructions on how to weave this fabric, see page 70.

Tutti-frutti

A customized cover for a plain notebook makes a unique gift, which will be treasured down the years. For instructions on how to weave this fabric, see page 86.

Weatherboard

Recycle all those old T-shirts and create some highly personal place mats. For instructions on how to weave this fabric, see page 88.

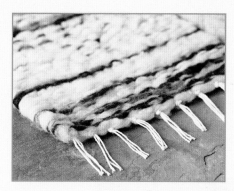

Rock

Try making this marvellous, pure fleece mat to put beside your bed. For instructions on how to weave this fabric, see page 94.

Ostrich

Drying your dishes will be a joy instead of a chore with these thick, smart tea towels. For instructions on how to weave this fabric, see page 96.

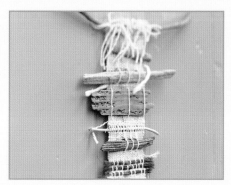

Beachcombing

Try out this intriguing way of saving and displaying the things you find on your summer holiday beach rambles. For instructions on how to weave this fabric, see page 102.

Cottage garden and Shell

Two cushions, one modern-looking made using ghiordes knotting and one classic-looking in natural shades. For instructions on how to weave these two fabrics, see pages 104 and 98.

glossary

Arc Weft thread curved in a half-moon shape between the warp threads before beating, to allow for take-up.

Balanced weave Warp and weft threads are equally visible in the finished fabric.

Beating Pushing down each row of the weft as you weave.

Color and weave Patterns made using two colors only, with numbered threading in plain weave.

Counting thread Waste yarn used to wrap the warp in measured groups while it is being wound on the warping board.

Cross The figure eight that is made at one end of the warp while it is measured on the warping board, to keep the threads in order.

Cross-sticks Used to spread out the warp and keep it in order while threading is taking place.

Dent The spacing system of the reed/rigid heddle. For example, a 10-dent heddle can be threaded with 10 warp ends per inch (2 cm) if one end is placed in every hole and slot.

Ends Individual lengths of warp threads.

Finger weaving A method of weaving by using the fingers to guide the weft through the warp threads.

Fleece The wool that is removed from the sheep's back after shearing.

Float patterns Made by using a pick-up stick with a rigid heddle.

Ghiordes knot Short lengths of fiber knotted around the warp threads in rows in between the rows of plain weave. Makes a tufted effect. Also known as a Turkish knot.

Header A narrow band of heavy yarn, string or rags woven in at the beginning of the weaving to space out the groups of warp threads.

Hopsack weave Yarn used double for both warp and weft.

Interlocking Wrapping the weft threads around each other on the selvedge to avoid loops and gaps.

Loom allowance The amount of warp added to the project length to allow for shrinkage and tying on.

Loom wastage The portion of warp behind the heddle, at the end of the weaving, which cannot be woven.

Peg loom Upright pegs set in a board around which the weft is woven.

Pick-up stick Flat wooden stick with one rounded end, used to pick up warp threads in some types of pattern weaving.

Plain weave The basic weave structure of over one, under one.

Ratchet A notched or toothed wheel on the side of the back and front rollers. Used to keep the warp threads under tension and to prevent the warp from unrolling.

Reed The reed spreads the warp threads to a particular sett, and different reeds are used to create light or heavy fabrics.

Reed hook A device with a hook at one end, used to pull the warp ends through the holes and slots.

Rigid heddle A frame containing plastic or metal bars, each of which has a hole in its center. The warp ends are threaded through the holes and slots. The rigid heddle lowers and raises the ends and is used to beat the weft into place.

Rovings A soft, rope-like fiber from which yarn is spun.

Selvedge The warpwise edge of the woven cloth.

Sett The number of warp ends per centimeter or inch.

Shed The V-shaped opening formed by raising and lowering the warp ends, through which the shuttle passes, carrying the weft thread.

Shuttle The tool that carries the weft thread.

Sliver A continuous strand of carded fibers, without twist.

Spaced and crammed warp Warp ends threaded double in some holes and slots and not in others.

Staple A naturally occurring single tuft of fleece.

Tabby Another name for the basic plain weave.

Take-up The amount by which the warp is shortened during the process of weaving.

Tension The degree of tightness to which the warp is stretched on the loom.

Ties Lengths of waste yarn used to tie the warps together before removing from the warping board.

Tops As rovings.

Warp Lengthwise threads that are held under tension on the loom.

Warp-faced Weaving where only the warp threads show because they are so close together.

Warping frame Wooden board with spaced pegs, around which a warp is measured and wound.

Warping pegs As above.

Weft Yarn woven crossways through the warp threads to make the cloth.

Weft-faced Weaving where only the weft threads show. The warp is spaced widely, so the weft slides down and covers it.

wpi/wpc Wraps per inch/wraps per centimetre.

international suppliers

The suppliers listed below will ship yarns and weaving equipment around the world.

www.ashford.co.nz
www.schachtspindle.com
www.louet.com
www.handweaversstudio.co.uk
www.pmwoolcraft.co.uk
www.fibrecrafts.com
www.winghamwools.co.uk
www.theyarntree.com
www.weavingworks.com
www.newvoyager.com

acknowledgments

The authors would like to thank Ashford Handicrafts Limited for the use of their Rigid Heddle Loom and Janet and Bill Hamilton of Anjay Fabrics for sourcing and supplying many of the yarns used in the projects.

index

Entries & page numbers in
italics indicate projects

credits

Editor **Camilla Davis**
Executive Art Editor **Leigh Jones**
Designer **Miranda Harvey**
Photographer **Vanessa Davies**
Illustrator **Sheilagh Noble**
Production Manager **Simone Nauerth**

Picture Acknowledgments
Special photography:
© Octopus Publishing Group Ltd/Vanessa Davies
Other photography:
Jupiterimages/Jules Cowan 58;
Leigh Jones 34, 42, 56, 74, 76, 100;
Photodisc 46, 66;
Rubberball Productions 64, 68.